Executive Summary for Solved II!

This book addresses Obamacare, Social Security Recipients, and Staggering Student Debts

Like its predecessor book Solved!, which deals with solutions for 60 million illegal residents in America, this book also has a unique structure. It consists of three different chapters taken from a book titled, *Top Ten American Political Books for 2018*. The three extracted chapters in this book (titles below) are synopses of three books I had written to solve three distinct problems that have been nagging Congressional Representatives of the people and Presidents for several years:

- Obamacare: A One-Line Repeal
- Boost Social Security Now!
- Wipe Out All Student Debt Now!

I0122220

The original full book titles shown above were written in the fall of 2017. The solutions described in these books solve (1) the problem of a government takeover of healthcare, (2) the problem of losing an entire generation of our best and brightest to student loan debt, and (3) The problem of government cheating on inflation, leading to the elderly at the door of the poorhouse.

Besides solving a big problem with illegal residents, a topic covered in the predecessor book Solved!, this book takes on three of the biggest challenges facing various segments of America at home today. I think you will see major value in the solutions.

Build a great campaign platform

Not only are the solutions that are outlined viable and cogent and designed to make America great again, they are also perfect for a national candidate for Congress or the US Senate. The constituencies are so large in all three solution areas that an advocate for these three solutions would be able to make short work of an entrenched incumbent politician who never chose to address these important problems.

Those citizens worried about Obamacare would opt out at a high level to keep their own plans. This would be a constituency of over

150,000,000 voters if Obamacare were repealed with one simple line. For Social Security recipients (SSR), offering a plan to boost the COLA to 15% per annum for any candidate would appeal to another huge constituency of 66 million. Finally, addressing the student debt crisis, which has a constituency of 48 billion is another big winner for any candidate who wants to win a national election.

Obamacare

The first problem on the list is #1 because over 54% of Americans say that the availability and affordability of healthcare is their #1 issue. Regardless of what Obama promised, you cannot keep your doctor and your healthcare plan with Obamacare. Worse than that, those with insurance through Obamacare, even without the individual mandate, can barely afford the policies. Worse than that, with the first health issue requiring the first huge deductible payment for a major illness, the patient on Obamacare without subsidies typically does not have enough in their meager budget to be pay the deductible. Deductibles are way too big for average people to afford. Obamacare is a disaster. The only ones who really like this program are those who have been helped by healthcare redistribution, which is simply a trick to get workers to pay for everybody's healthcare including their own.

The American taxpayers, many of whom cannot pay their own health insurance, are coerced into paying for over 10 million other people who had been making too much money to qualify for Medicaid for many years. Democrats, hoping to gain their votes added coverage for them to Obamacare via stipends paid by you and I.

It is simply healthcare redistribution. Those who had healthcare pre-Obama, can no longer afford it and those who did not qualify, now are enjoying Obamacare stipends paid by Americans who now cannot afford their own healthcare.

Ending the Obamacare standoff would stage any challenger for a national public office for a big win. Obamacare has proven unaffordable for those who do not receive huge government / taxpayer funded subsidies. Obamacare is a good deal for only the 10

Solved II!

Unsolvable Domestic problems—Obamacare, Social Security, Student Debt—solved right here.

We did our part in bringing the best domestic solutions for Obamacare, Social Security, and staggering student debt to you in their full versions and now again in this mini-sampling of the Whitman's Sampler / CliffsNotes-like versions. In each of the three chapters of this mini sampler, you'll find a book purpose section followed by an introduction, followed by a Preface and a few chapters of each original book.

To differentiate chapters of the mini sampler book from the about books, we use a Ch designator rather than Chapter, followed by the Chapter number. That's all we need right here for an intro. Here are the titles of three solution books for Obamacare, Seniors & Social Security, and Student Debt. These are part of the recently released book titled Top Ten American Political Books for 2018. Enjoy! The books in this mini-sampler are highlighted below in bold.

1. Taxation Without Representation Fourth Edition– Can the U.S. avoid another "Boston Tea Party?"
2. DELETE the EPA! EPA agenda is not to save human lives. Is its insidious goal world population control?
3. Deport All Millennials Now! It ought to be easy. They'll line up like it's a free vacation
4. No Free Lunch—Pay Back Welfare The first book that recommends that welfare should not be free money
5. **Wipe Out All Student Debt Now! Unique solutions to the $1.45 Trillion debt accumulation**
6. **Boost Social Security Now!   A solution to get Seniors out of the poorhouse; Hey buddy, can you spare a dime?**
7. Legalizing Illegal Aliens Via Resident Visas A great Americans-first plan which saves $trillions. Learn how!
8. Pay-To-Go--An America-first immigration fix. No more deportations, except for bad guys
9. **Obamacare: A One-Line Repeal   Congress must get this done.**
10. 60 Million Illegals in America!!! A simple, America-first solution!

BRIAN W. KELLY

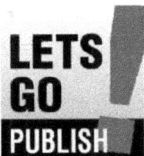

Solved II

Editor	Brian P. Kelly
Author	Brian W. Kelly

Disclaimer: Though judicious care was taken throughout the writing and the publication of this work that the information contained herein is accurate, there is no expressed or implied warranty that all information in this book is 100% correct. Therefore, neither LETS GO PUBLISH, nor the author accepts liability for any use of this work.

Trademarks: A number of products and names referenced in this book are trade names and trademarks of their respective companies.

Referenced Material: *The information in this book has been obtained through personal and third-party observations, interviews, and copious research. Where unique information has been provided or extracted from other sources, those sources are acknowledged within the text of the book itself or at the end of the chapter in the Sources Section. Thus, there are no formal footnotes nor is there a bibliography section. Any picture that does not have a source was taken from various sites on the Internet with no credit attached. If resource owners would like credit in the next printing, please email publisher.*

Published by: LETS GO PUBLISH!
Publisher: Brian P. Kelly
Editor: Brian P. Kelly
P.O Box 621   Wilkes-Barre, PA   www.letsgopublish.com

Library of Congress Copyright Information Pending
Book Cover Design by B. W. Kelly;
Editing and original writing by B. P. Kelly

ISBN Information: The International Standard Book Number (ISBN) is a *unique machine-readable identification number, which marks any book unmistakably. The ISBN is the clear standard in the book industry. 159 countries and territories are officially ISBN members. The Official ISBN for this book is also on the outside cover:* **978-1-947402-34-8**

The price for this work is: **$8.95 USD**

10   9   8   7   6   5   4   3   2   1

Release Date: January 2018 million who get theirs via government stipends. It is a small constituency and most in that group do not vote anyway. No candidate ever got elected by people who do not vote.

Yet, there is a huge constituency of over 150 million voters that the press ignores. They do not have Obamacare and they do not want to give up employer-provided insurance to have it. You can take a poll on that.

The Obamacare pollsters offer fake news in their polling results. What their polls don't show or attempt to differentiate is that those voters who actually have to buy their insurance on the Obamacare marketplaces are very unhappy. They may be able to afford the insurance, but they cannot afford the high deductibles when they get sick.

The happy ones for Obamacare in the national polls are not signed up for Obamacare and do not want it. They get their insurance through their work, get it via Medicaid, or are over 65 and have guaranteed coverage through Medicare. It would be a major trauma for over 150 million voters, including the Congress if they were forced to be on Obamacare to be forced to trade in whatever they have for Obamacare.

If the questions in the positive polling reflected those kind of answers, truth might even come from the polls. The bottom line is that Obamacare is not a good deal for anybody not qualifying for a huge subsidy. For those who are not in the subsidy category, they ought to want it gone so they can get whatever they want to stay secure.

This upside-down system of healthcare must be repealed. There should be no government replacement. Keep government out of the general healthcare market. Repeal Obamacare with a one-line repeal. Back to marketplace basics. A great candidate would make sure that with Obamacare as a national option, one day those happy with what they have may have to change and they would not like that one bit.

Social Security

After healthcare and the economy, which is now being solved by the Trump administration and the new tax plan, the next biggest concern of Americans is the Social Security System. Some are concerned as they worry that it might not be able to sustain itself while others see the government cheating on the cost of living increases (CPI). While seniors are losing their homes and many, for want of bread and milk, are on the verge of heading to the poorhouse, Congress recently pretended to give a 2% raise for 2018 but then snatched it right back.

For most, if not all seniors, the "generous" 2% increase (when Wilkes-Barre City employees all received 3% raises), was all swallowed up by increased Medicare Part B premiums.

As an example of the plight of seniors, let me explain Medicare Part B and its detrimental effect on seniors' SSR "raises" The quotes on raises are intentional. Medicare Part B is optional insurance that really is needed by almost all seniors, other than those who are rich. That is simple enough.

If I know that, then the government and your Congress know that also but for some reason they do not care an iota. Part B (Medical Insurance) covers most medically necessary doctors' services, preventive care, durable medical equipment, hospital outpatient services, laboratory tests, x-rays, mental health care, and some home health and ambulance services. Who living today, young or old does not need these services? Yet the government does not include these in the CPI calculation so that sick seniors are almost condemned to die or go on welfare if they can get it.

Most seniors pay a monthly premium for this coverage which comes out of their social security payments. It is an expense just like bread, milk and tuna cat food. In calculating the CPI, the Bureau of Labor statistics gives no credit for either the medical procedures covered by Part B nor for the Part B premium itself as paid by seniors. Yet, after paying these expenses, seniors have less money for bread and milk and rent and taxes and small gifts from the Dollar Store for the grandkids.

Yes, these are part of the things a senior citizen views as part of their cost of living—not a mythical cost of living created by bureaucrats and coffee-breath professors. The goal of the bureaucrats is to fraudulently take back the annual raises to SS recipients How is it not part of the cost of living and why is it not included? It should be.

After I got done paying for my Part B this year, there was no SSR raise at all left for my family's needs nor for any other SSR recipient's family's needs. .Who cares? Few! Additionally, my AARP Medigap insurance went up in 2018 also and there was none of that huge 2% raise left to pay for that either. So, how did I, or any of the other 62 million SSR recipients get a real raise in 2018. We did not. Instead we all fell further behind the proverbial eight-ball.

What is a poorhouse?

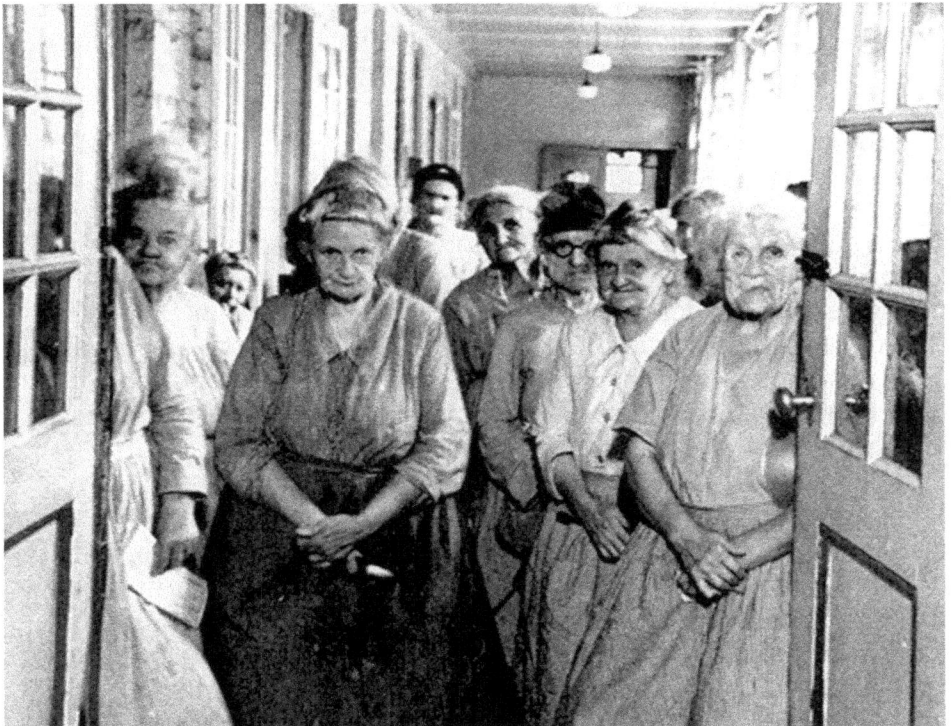

The door to the poorhouse was the main form of economic security for many elderly Americans in the days before Social Security.

Before social security, poorhouses most certainly existed. They were tax-supported residential institutions to which people were required to go if they could not support themselves. They were started as a method of providing a less expensive (to the taxpayers) alternative to what we would now days call "welfare" - what was called "outdoor relief" in those days. People requested help from the community

Overseer of the Poor (sometimes also called a Poor Master) - an elected town official.

If the need was great or likely to be long-term, people were shipped to the poorhouse instead of being given relief while they continued to live independently. Sometimes they were sent there even if they had not requested help from the Overseer of the Poor. That was usually done when they were found guilty of begging in public, or perhaps not paying debts to important people, etc. Despite how it might seem, these "houses" were not technically "debtors' prisons." Someone could owe a great deal of money, but if they could still provide themselves with the necessities for remaining independent, they might avoid the poorhouse. Our grandparents feared the poorhouse and often talked about it.

Poorhouses began to disappear after the enactment of the Social Security Act in 1935 and completely vanished in the1950s with the exception a few institutions run by churches that emphasized giving one a hand up, not a handout. Unfortunately for today's times, most of these faith-based institutions have closed because it is hard to compete with a federal government that hands out money, food, health care and a host of other services for doing absolutely nothing. But, many seniors are proud and want to avoid the modern poorhouse (welfare) at all costs, and so they barely subsist on their SSR wages and they seek no welfare.

The sages of government are unfortunately more interested in reducing the government debt than helping seniors live acceptably. Years ago, about 1980 or so, the government began to cheat on the consumer price index. They figured if they lied about the inflation rate, with some hocus pocus nonsense, then they would not have to give accurate yearly cost of living raises to SSR recipients. A one-time Head of the Fed suggested a CPI modification that was embraced by the government and the coffee-breath academicians as being the way to cheat seniors without us knowing about it. I bet he never stoked down his fire to save energy because he could afford the full cost of 24X7 heat.

Michael Boskin, a one-time chief economist to the first Bush Administration, and Alan Greenspan, Chairman of the Board of Governors of the Federal Reserve System. concocted a dandy scheme to stiff seniors early in the Clinton Administration. Until Boskin and Greenspan got involved, the consumer price index (CPI) was measured using the costs of a fixed basket of goods, a fairly simple and straightforward concept. The identical basket of goods would be priced at prevailing market costs for each period, and the period-to-period change in the cost of that market basket represented the rate of inflation in terms of maintaining a constant standard of living. That is fair. But it was too fair for Greenspan and Boskin, as it resulted in seniors having to receive annual COLA increases based on the actual increasing cost of living.

The true market basket was not good enough for those without concern for seniors' standard of living. Boskin and Alan Greenspan argued that when steak got too expensive, the consumer would substitute hamburger for the steak, and that the inflation measure should reflect the costs tied to buying hamburger versus steak. Eventually, it became OK for the bureaucrats to replace hamburger with less expensive tuna and eventually because the protein value was the same, cat tuna replaced regular tuna in the market basket. White albacore was too pricey to make the market basket.

Besides this, whenever a measurable item such as in the 1970's with the increasing price of oil, made it seem like seniors would get too much in their annual cost of living increment, government would take out that item from the market basket and never reinsert it to save the government money even though seniors had to pay the increased price of gas and whatever else was removed from the basket

Ironically health insurance, such as Medicare part B is not in the basket for a check on inflation. And, so as noted, the government "gives" 2% for 2018, and in lockstep, Medicare Part B takes that 2% right back Thus seniors absorb all of the other elements of inflation out of their prior amounts.

The big Whigs all know about the ruse but choose to ignore it. They joke about it, but it is no joke. For example, a 1970's economic commentator Barry Ritholtz has joked that core inflation (Greenspan style) is better called "inflation ex-inflation"—i.e., inflation after the inflation has been excluded.) Think about that and you can see that the deception of seniors has been intentional, and it continues with a new notion called the chained CPI that will cost seniors even more.

If you look at the original precepts of social security with a required annual kicker for increases in the cost of living, as part of the contract with the workers of the day, in essence the government has stolen right from the pockets of seniors by denying them a fair cost of living increase. Yet, nobody in government has been brave enough to tell seniors, who are losing their homes in droves, and who are being made "poorhouse ready," about any of this chicanery.

Institutionalized lying is OK now for those in government. By anybody's measures who seek the truth, the numbers for the CPI are off by at least 125% from what would have been calculated if pre-1980 standards were applied. The fact that the error is cumulative; viz. that each year's gap is compounded by the following year makes the pain on seniors even more severe. Another example is that as of November 2008, the true CPI had risen by 13% in that year. Yet, the Bureau of Labor Statistics listed inflation at 3.8%. Seniors had to prepare for a COLA increase that was 9.2% less than their cost for required items from the markets where they shopped.

Walter E Williams, an American blessing, who operates the shadowstats.com site, proves that seniors have been stiffed by much more than just 125%. Williams proves that seniors should be making 4½ times what their dollars were worth in 1980. Thet's $450 instead of $100.00. Any senior would love to have a small proportion of that.

As intimated earlier in this section, there is a new disinformation program that has been adopted by the government at the end of 2017. The new notion is called the chained CPI. It is now being used as the methodology for the CPI and it should prove even more difficult for seniors, Whatever it once was, it is worse.

Since it would be difficult to give any huge increase to seniors needed to rectify this situation caused by government thievery, all at once, my recommendation is that we approach it gradually. For the next four years, the COLA should be 15% each year plus the real cost of living. That ought to be enough to remove seniors from the on-deck circle directly outside the poorhouse.

Student Debt

Four in ten Americans believe that President Trump's administration should forgive all federal student debt in order to help stimulate the economy, according to a new survey revealed in 2017. As time goes by as more Americans realize we are excluding a full generation of Americans in our economy, this number will increase from a simple majority to an overwhelming endorsement of wiping out this nasty and unfair debt as soon as possible.

This debt exists because of major mistakes by government and academic institutions. There are lots of ways to pay for this generous notion by American citizens and all of them are good. No American can want a full generation of Americans to be left behind in the Trump economy. We need this debt wiped out now and we need safeguards so that pimple-faced seventeen-year-olds can never again sign up for a life in a debtor's prison.

According to MoneyTips.com, attitudes have changed from a time when Americans thought college students should be punished for making bad choices to today, when we need 48 million new spenders in our economy. The spenders with the greatest potential to spend today are not spending because of student debt.

Unlike DACA children, these kids are really kids, at least they were when they were snookered to join academia for a *can't miss* college degree. Moreover, they are American kids, not foreigners. They were sucked into bad things by greedy admission counsellors at universities and loan sharks, with no help from a damning Congress. Nearly 42% of Americans today agree or strongly agree that the government should wipe out all debt, while less than 37% disagree or strongly disagree with that move, and the remaining 21% neither agree nor disagree.

We all can have winning bets that there are lots better solutions to the problem of seventeen and eighteen-year-olds having been persuaded to dig huge financial holes in their lives with no escape so that they could attend college. Somehow, the same banks or financial aid offices that throw money at these "kids," would not loan a 17-year-old enough to buy a popsicle, a bike, or a car and certainly not a house on their best business days. Yet they were willing to loan a house-worth of cash, so a kid could go to college. Why?

Because they knew if they suckered the kid in, the government funded by the taxpayers would bail all the kids out one at a time, and the tuition check would be long cashed. We do need to get something back from universities for the unfulfilled promises.

They don't promise a job after four years when they take that $100,000 from any "kid." They don't even promise a degree. Worse than that, they don't promise anything close in value to its $100,000 price tag. They promise nothing. No wonder one out of six student borrowers default today when the time comes to pay back the loan. And, the rate of defaults is getting even worse. The irony is that the "kids" never even thought that the loans needed to be paid back. Nobody at the university ever thought to tell them that it was not a gift.

I once thought this problem could be solved by a combination of lower interest rates, some forgiveness, etc. I no longer think such a piecemeal plan is the correct solution. Why did I change my perspective?

I fear that an entire generation of students, mostly millennials, will be lost and will never be found again unless drastic action is taken now. And so, I call for legislation that wipes out all student debt now. It is not a one-way benefit like giving welfare to illegal aliens. Wait until you see what such a kind act from America will do to boost the US economy beyond even our current expectations. In the book from which this information is extracted, I offer some great ways in which we can pay for the write-off of the student debt without hurting taxpayers and without putting banks under.

Can you imagine if instead of gifts to crony capitalists such as Solyndra, Obama eliminated student debt? Obama would not have known why, but his economy would have sky-rocketed unexpectedly just like today. If we do this, the economy will hit the moon. Independent of that, as Americans, we must do the right thing to save a full generation of student graduates who have had to endure the highest tuition rates as well as the loan sharks who pushed the notion of accepting them as a good thing.

One hundred years ago, I would be arguing for high schools to offer student forgiveness if the US had not determined to educate our 12 to 18-year-olds from taxpayer revenues. Should we punish our next generation so much that we lose them, and that foreigners who got stipends and tokens of appreciation for diversity purposes get the jobs our kids should have?

President Trump knows a ripoff & a rigged system

President Trump in understandable terms has netted out the student debt crisis from both a student and parent perspective: "They go, and they work, and they take loans, and they're borrowed up, and they can't breathe, and they get through college and the worst thing is, they go through that whole process and they don't have any job." Trump has it right, and worse than that, when the US system hurts them, our best and brightest lose hope.

The book title *Wipe Out Student Debt Now*, which is mini-highlighted in this book, addresses the massive $1.45 Trillion student debt already on the books and it presents a boldly unique plan to assure that students with loans have a chance of success with a job of their choice. Isn't it about time?

This action will kick start the economy with such a punch that Americans will be talking about how great it is that America is so great again. Additionally, it will bring back a whole generation of lost souls with no chance in life—the millennials—so they can lead normal lives like all other generations before them.

It helps to recall that President Obama increased the National Debt by $9.1 Trillion in just eight years, hoping to assure that illegal aliens had all the resources they needed to take as many American jobs as they could. He just about doubled our debt and has nothing to show for his efforts. Tell me where the money went? It was spent but what good did it do?

What if we had taken a small piece of that expenditure and paid off all student debt? Wow! What if at the same time so it never happens again, we put in measures to assure that 17-year-olds could never be sucked into giving up the promise of a real life for a fake-news promise by university officials of prosperity-- ever, ever again.

It is too bad that our former president did not have the foresight to use $1.45 Trillion of that wasteful largesse to help America. With less than 15% of this reckless, aimless crony capitalist spending, the former president could have been a folk hero among many Americans.

He could have and should have spent more wisely and wiped out 100% of the student debt now strangling our young American adults and holding the US economy hostage. Until the student debt crisis is put behind us, the most physically capable and more than likely, the brightest people in America, our recent college graduates, between the ages of twenty and forty, will not be part of the American game of life. We will lose an entire generation of Americans.

Can you imagine?

Without a spectacular, magnanimous act by the Congress and the President, we will lose an entire generation of great Americans to student loan debt. As Americans, do we really want that as our historical legacy?

Preface:

Brian W. Kelly enjoyed putting this mini-sampler book together. Being the author of each of the ten books, which outline the major solutions for the severe domestic ills afflicting America today, made it easy for Brian to pick and choose the synopses that would be in this Whitman's Sampler / CliffsNotes version highlighting solutions for Obamacare, Social Security, and Student Debt.

Brian's objective was to put in one condensed book the many solutions that have evaded the best of the best in Congress and the presidency for many years for one reason or another. Brian believes he did the job for Congress if we can get them to read the book. A secondary objective for Kelly was that he hoped that when any of the "CliffsNotes" versions were read, the reader would believe they had gotten the full picture of both the problem and the solution, even though the Whitman's Sampler synopsis would not contain all of the supporting detail.

Kelly is very happy that he was able to achieve both objectives.

Why did Brian W. Kelly write this book?

Brian W. Kelly saw the major problems with Obamacare unaffordability, Social Security recipients headed for the poorhouse, and student debt ready to wipe out a generation of Americans, keeping them from experiencing the American dream.

Brian loves America and like President Trump, he wants America to be great because great Americans, who are permitted to live without government constraints, are the vehicle which will make America and all Americans great again.

You will love this book because three of the most pressing domestic problems that America faces are solved within the short mini Whitman's Sampler / CliffsNotes versions of the detailed solutions.

Thank you for being so nice as to purchase this book and for helping keep America the only place in the living world where freedom matters more than anything else.

I wish you the best.

Brian P. Kelly, Publisher
Wilkes-Barre, Pennsylvania

Table of Contents – Mini Sampler:

Chapter numbers above refer to the #s in the sequence of the original books.

About the Author

Brian W. Kelly retired as an Assistant Professor in the Business Information Technology (BIT) program at Marywood University, where he also served as the IBM i and Midrange Systems Technical Advisor to the IT Faculty. Kelly designed, developed, and taught many college and professional courses. He continues as a contributing technical editor to a number of IT industry magazines, including "The Four Hundred" and "Four Hundred Guru," published by IT Jungle.

Kelly is a former IBM Senior Systems Engineer and IBM Mid Atlantic Area Specialist. His specialty was designing applications for customers as well as implementing advanced IBM operating systems and software facilities on their machines.

He has an active information technology consultancy. He is the author of 148 books and numerous technical articles. Kelly has been a frequent speaker at COMMON, IBM conferences, and other technical conferences.

Brian was a candidate for US Congress from Pennsylvania in 2010 and he brings a lot of experience to his writing endeavors. Brian Kelly knows how to solve most of the domestic problems in the US. Let's hope the Congress hears him out.

Chapter 1 Great Domestic Solutions Ready for 2018

The chapter was written by Brian Patrick Kelly, the author's oldest son, to help kickoff this memorable book. Enjoy!

Writing books can be fun

Prolific author Brian Kelly produces so many books in a given year even his family cannot explain how he does it. His most popular books throughout the years, such as Great Moments in Alabama Football, have focused primarily on sports themes, but that is not his original claim to fame. Kelly's initial prior experience was problem solving in information technology and later political diagnosis and remedies. His U.S. domestic policy recommendations are second to none.

Anyone in the patriotic or conservative world who finds themselves flirting with finding an innovative solution to the domestic ills that have been eluding supposed experts for far too long will find their needs more than satisfied by one of Kelly's refreshing works. For open minded liberals or progressives, many of his answers can be hung on either side of the aisle.

Kelly's solutions are deceptively simple and occasionally counterintuitive at first glance. One's first question may be, "Can something so simple actually solve the problem?" After reading further and understanding his proposals, Kelly aspires to allow a new world of thought to unfold before the eyes and instill the positive belief that many of the nation's seemingly intractable maladies are indeed curable.

Historically, great thinkers and influential problem solvers possess an uncanny ability to translate otherwise arduous complex notions into language that any audience can readily understand. Kelly prides himself on cutting through argument, debate and doubt, and offers solutions that all can process and appreciate. Brian's plain talk solutions are authentic, cogent, clear, and palpable, quite unlike rocket science. He reveals a logical path for readers that culminate in "Of course!" rather than "What?!"

Brian has been quietly solving domestic problems for many years with various iterations of books that in 2017 have all been fine-tuned to meet the needs of today. Even his early books, such as No Taxation Without Representation, were considered groundbreaking. The 2017 editions of all of Kelly's books written to solve America's most urgent domestic issues are his most refined yet.

His readers are continually amazed that a layman who spent his life as a technician for IBM could redeploy his analytical and problem-solving skills to the broader challenges facing America. He has accomplished this repeatedly and in 2017, he has done it again by preparing the fixes that the Congress and the President can deploy in 2018.

With this book of synopses, Brian Kelly now has one hundred and forty-six books to his credit. They vividly describe various aspects of American life. A good many of Kelly's 2017 books specify how the nation can address its many challenges in the current century.

While Kelly may allocate personal time to offering advice on issues like how many crossing guards are needed at a local intersection in Wilkes-Barre, Pennsylvania, he does not purport to be an expert on such matters which he has not yet studied in depth. By contrast, Kelly has spent years contemplating the major social and domestic problems in the United States and finds himself peerless in his insight.

To remain adept, Kelly perpetually studies the major domestic issues of our time and examines and reexamines potential sensible solutions. He ran for U.S. Congress as a Democrat in 2010, adhering to his vow to take no campaign donations in 2010 and was pleased to receive 17% of the vote despite being vastly outspent and having little prior name recognition.

He understood the system to be rigged against ordinary Americans like himself who are not indentured to a major donor with plenty of reserve funds and harbored no illusions of overnight success. Kelly is not for purchase; his merit lies in diagnosis and rectification of problems.

Increasingly, more Democrats such as Brian are beginning to realize that the entrenched class, also known as "the Swamp," has control over everything consequential in the U.S. except for the often-misdirected voting power of the people. Though we still retain control of the government to some extent, we often fail to correctly exercise our power. Kelly believes that even the few crumbs and inches gained are only acquired once those gains have been predetermined by the powers to be worthless. Like many of you, he opposes our domination by this Swamp.

Like Donald Trump, your author wants to make America great again. Not being president of course, makes it a lot more difficult to insert real solutions into the political mix of today. Brian Kelly is your average normal guy but for one difference. In his role as the most published non-fiction author in America, Kelly has built a solution for each of the most pressing domestic US issues of today.

For each problem, Kelly has at least one book in his arsenal that solves the problem. Sometimes it takes two and sometimes even more than two books to completely solve the most nagging issues.

Brian Kelly writes, and he writes, and he thinks, and he articulates. But, as a normal, regular American; he has no power or resources to force his ideas upon anyone. It is not an easy task.

Even Donald Trump as CEO of America is having problems dislodging the gunk and muck in the Swamp and getting his agenda implemented. The Swamp dwellers have lots of spare cash to fight all comers. The Establishment has many people to whom they pay large sums to fight for them every day. For that, the political junkies in the SWAMP get the best advice about how to keep the President at bay.

Brian Kelly's major domestic solutions are contained in his books. Ten books unfortunately to solve ten major problems provides a lot of material for solutions. Consequently, it is too much reading all at once for even the best of us. And, so, the purpose of this "Whitman's Sampler" book of synopses, is to be a book of books, written in "CliffsNotes" style for easy reading and comprehending.

The book is titled: *Top Ten American Political Books for 2018*. It provides a comprehensive set of summaries on the best approaches to tackle the major domestic US issues that we are facing in 2018. It is designed to be read one chapter at a time in a short period so that Americans can have a big win for the country. When the right people read this set of "CliffsNotes" books and begin to pass laws and implement the plans contained herein, America will be well on its way to greatness again, working to achieve independence from those keeping us down.

Brian Kelly is not a total cynic but a realist like many lifelong Democrats whose disgust with established special interests has made them gravitate towards the countermeasure of Donald Trump. Why should ordinary people volunteer to be pushed around by dishonest Democrats anymore? Despite being a billionaire, Trump relates to the people in a way that breaks through the authoritarian forced politeness behind which masquerades the nefarious interests of the entrenched political class.

Donald Trump takes no salary as he finds being a great president as reward enough for his daily toil. Even as he is constantly assailed by our disingenuous and certifiably fake news media, he dusts himself off and goes right back at it the next day on behalf of all of us.

Democrats have failed their original vision of a world where families can earn a decent wage by working, opting instead to reward their anti-American donors who prey on the very people the Party was founded to help prosper. Democrats want the people to believe that their captured government should be sufficient for the people's needs, having done their best to extinguish any members who otherwise would be driven to work on behalf of the population at large.

One of the greatest challenges President Trump faces is how to rehabilitate faith in our system, when the Democratic Party, a once reliable bedrock institution, is now bitterly distrusted. We all wish him well on that account.

So, what does someone without Mr. Trump's resources do? Most of us cannot afford to run a successful campaign but are united in our goal of *Making America Great Again*. Kelly hopes his ideas can influence the nation and President Trump personally, as though they both lack pure omniscience, they share a powerful intellect, heart of gold, and desire to restore America to its former glory.

Kelly has some great ideas. He increasingly sells more and more books each month but because he currently lacks fame, his solutions have yet to reach a widespread audience that could one day promote the policies that ultimately reach the President's desk. He writes, thinks, and articulates, knowing full well that his ideas' path to fruition is an indirect one. While Mr. Trump has the power and influence to accomplish many of his plans for the nation, Brian understands that his ideas are going nowhere unless they are put into action prompted by popular will and executed by the President's pen.

As noted previously, the road ahead is difficult. Even Donald Trump himself is having problems dislodging the sludge and serpentine slugs in the dreaded swamp who have full control of America. They are able to spare any expense to protect their system of chicanery at all costs, including paid lackeys in the media who defend the indefensible.

They are well organized and protected. Another lever in the system of revolving doors include the overpaid consultants who provide inside access to electoral success. For many of the most venal knaves in office purporting to be public servants, re-election of course is a vanity success for its own sake, rather than enabling a better life for the citizens of this country.

So, what does Brian Kelly have to offer? This book provides a good overview. Titled *Top Ten American Political Books for 2018*, it is a synopsis on the best approaches to tackle domestic US issues in 2018 for Americans to finally achieve success in the country.

Nothing in life worth having is easy and the only thing once can do alone in life is fail. And, so, Brian Kelly has had a good friend for the last six years, Congressman Lou Barletta who also hails from Northeastern Pennsylvania and currently serves as its representative. Kelly and Barletta became friends when Kelly ran for Congress, lost in the primary, and asked Barletta how he could help him win his Congressional seat.

Kelly continually communicates with and meets with the Congressman to discuss his ideas for the improvement America. The Congressman is always warm and engaging and Kelly hopes to demonstrate enough popular political will to move forward with his policy ideas. Kelly believes the Congressman is the real deal, so to speak, so he continues to raise awareness of these issues in his presence as he believes it to be one of the best avenues to reach President Trump.

Brian supports this Congressman in 2018 for his next big strategic operation—a run for the US Senate. Pennsylvania currently has one of the ineptest Senators representing the state in Pennsylvania history. Bob Casey Jr. a nice enough guy from Scranton, is regarded as but a shadow of the towering figure his father was, when the senior Casey served as Governor of Pennsylvania.

Most people in the local area gave up hope on Casey Jr. a long time ago, as he revealed himself to be little more than a water-carrier for Barack Obama and then Hillary Clinton in her notoriously corrupt failed bid for President in 2016.

To put Casey in perspective, when he first ran for the U.S. Senate, a Philadelphia Inquirer columnist wrote that Casey's *make-no-waves style* was as exciting as "oatmeal." Considering the Inquirer's center-left editorial bias, the fact that this was the most positive thing they could muster was a surprise to even Democrats.

Brian Kelly wrote this new compendium book so that between the covers of just one book, he is now able to introduce the precepts that are detailed in all ten books released in 2017. In this way, policy makers and interested citizens alike can have an even more concise tool from which to create the legislation necessary to disinfect the United States of the major issues that are keeping the country from moving forward without impediment.

By way of a list, as a topical introduction, these are the major domestic issues for which Brian Kelly has fashioned the most appropriate solutions for 2008.

- ✓ Saving millennials so they do not become the lost generation
- ✓ Refranchise student borrowers
- ✓ Prescribes how colleges and universities can become more honest in promising the world to 17-year-old high school kids, and locking them in to huge debt
- ✓ Remove welfare as a free lunch
- ✓ Ending healthcare redistribution
- ✓ Provide Social Security recipients with a COLA that makes up for past inaccuracies
- ✓ Provide a no-amnesty, no cost, pro-American rescue of illegal aliens from the shadows.
- ✓ Provide cash for self-deportation of illegal aliens
- ✓ Provide cash for self-deportation of anchor babies
- ✓ Provide cash for self-deportation of two-term green card holders.
- ✓ Provide no amnesty; no way!
- ✓ Provide a system so that Americans have first opportunities for every job that comes available.
- ✓ Save well over $500 billion per year on immigration costs
- ✓ Repeal Obamacare with a market, not a government replacement.
- ✓ Downsize the EPA by 95%
- ✓ Avoid Taxation Without Representation

The solutions written in the latter part of 2017 are contained in Brian Kelly's ten books that are outlined in this book titled, *Top Ten American Political Books for 2018* and the solutions are primed to help America with its domestic problem set for 2018.   The books are listed in reverse order of publishing date. The book titles contain solutions for tall of the above listed problems.

The Top Ten Political Books in America for 2018 are as follows:

- Taxation Without Representation Fourth Edition--Can the U.S. Avoid Another "Boston Tea Party?"

- DELETE the EPA! EPA agenda is not to save human lives. Is its insidious goal world population control?
- Deport All Millennials Now! It ought to be easy. They'll line up like it's a free vacation
- No Free Lunch—Pay Back Welfare The first book that recommends that welfare should not be free money
- Wipe Out All Student Debt Now! Unique solutions to the $1.45 Trillion debt accumulation
- Boost Social Security Now! A solution to get Seniors out of the poorhouse; Hey buddy, can you spare a dime?
- Legalizing Illegal Aliens Via Resident Visas-- A great Americans-first plan which saves $Trillions. Learn how!
- Pay-To-Go-- An America-first immigration fix No more deportations
- Obamacare: A One-Line Repeal Congress must get this done
- 60 Million Illegals in America!!! A simple, America-first solution!

Thank you,
Brian Patrick Kelly
Editor in Chief & Publisher of Lets Go Publish! Publishers.

Chapter 10 Obamacare: A One-Line Repeal

Obamacare: A One-Line Repeal
Brian W. Kelly

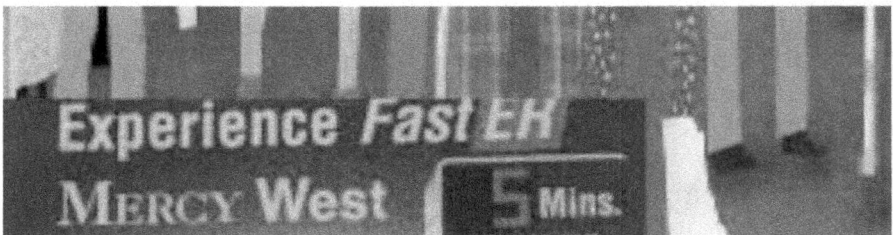

Congress must get this done!

Book purpose:

Most Americans looked at the idea of repeal and replace Obamacare as a really simple notion. Unfortunately, the *replace* part was not well understood by the people. It was intentional chicanery by the government so that Republicans would get credit for repealing Obamacare while putting back a system that was in fact Obamacare with just a few changes. Most Americans paying attention did not like the bait and switch pulled on us by officials in the Republican Party.

Therefore, we are still looking for a one-line repeal. Just repeal it! Get it done. None of us, who lost our former healthcare to Obama chicanery, care about a replacement. Go back to whatever the laws were in existence when Obamacare became effective. It is OK if **after** the big repeal, to get some touch up work done such as keeping kids on policies until they are 26 and some guarantees about not being dropped by a carrier and something fair about preexisting conditions. The repeal should be one line and that one line must take away everything including the death panels.

Polls propping up Obamacare are lies just like Obamacare has always been a lie

Despite what Democrats wanting to make former President Obama into a modern saint will say; most thinking Americans hate Obamacare. Why is that? The answer is simple, Americans have worked for healthcare since the Roosevelt days and they do not want the government in charge of their healthcare. Yes, it is that simple, but Congress, who made themselves immune to the effects of Obamacare does not share their pain.

an end to

President Trump is flirting with the idea of ending Congress' illegal gravy train of subsidies that pay for their health care premiums. These are illegal subsidies which the Congress takes because they are special. They are valued at roughly $6,000 for an individual policy, and $12,000 for a family policy. They are paid to the approximately 12,000 members and staff who purchase their health care insurance on the District of Columbia small business exchange. No Virginia, you cannot purchase your healthcare from the DC small business exchange.

The same Congress that says there is only one way for Americans to get healthcare gets theirs a different way. These subsidy payments are a direct violation of not just the spirit, but the letter of the Affordable Care Act, which required Members and their staffs to leave their generous Federal Employee Health Benefit Program plans and instead purchase their health insurance through the Obamacare exchanges. How can these hypocrites deny Americans the same rights as they take themselves on healthcare—a free market?

Americans have a quiet fear as they give up their rights to first-class healthcare for Obamacare, that the guy who gets all the political jobs in their neighborhood will be designated as the guy who determines whether they get treatment or not, and what is covered.

Health insurance gained by getting a good job and working hard to keep it no longer will matter. Johnny B. Good, the guy who put up the spite fence next door to you—the guy with the four Pit Bulls, will cup his hands to his face after you make your plea, and then he will decide if your operation is needed. Your money won't matter when Johnny from the Neighborhood is in charge. That thought alone scares Americans to death.

Americans are not happy with Obamacare's increasing premium costs and its increasing out-of-reach deductibles, and they don't like that doctors are dropping out of Obamacare like flies giving decreased access to health professionals. Americans know what they don't like. We don't like Obamacare, period. Repeal it or pay at the ballot box.

Americans also know what they do like. They know that they do not want the government, especially neighborhood guys like Johnny B. Good making health decisions for their family. I

applaud the efforts of good and honest US representatives willing
to put a steel tip on their shoe and boot Obamacare out of town for
good.

President Trump intrinsically knows how to do business logically
without convoluted rules. The plan outlined right here in this book
shows how our wonderful President can use the simplest
methodology ever to repeal and replace Obamacare with a market
based solution—exactly the way he promised during the
campaign.

I predict that you will read this book from cover to cover in one
sitting.

Why do people hate Obamacare?

Few people today trust the polls that are continually being
reported by both the real and the fake news media. So, when those
who hate Obamacare just nose out those who love Obamacare
when just 10 million people are on Obamacare out of a country-
full, it does not add up. People see a failed program that stinks of
politics and government control and unless they get theirs for free,
they want it gone and fast. Of course having a corrupt press that
still protects Obama's legacy does not help the bulk of the
American people.

Most of my friends just roll their eyes at ne mention of the word
Obamacare. This is often followed by a bunch of negative phrases.

Though from what I see, it is worse than the polling results, which
are not positive for Obamacare. About 40% of Americans held an
unfavorable opinion of the law in April 2010, while 46% had a
favorable view. This poll was by a Kaiser Family Foundation poll
who for whatever reason always report Obamacare in a positive
light.

Since the original polling, the public's perception has generally
been less positive and recently the numbers are more like 45% of
the people having a negative view, versus 43% with a positive one.
To me, if this is accurate, it can only be a poll of the uninformed
by the biased.

We all know that Donald Trump promised a swift *repeal of Obamacare* and this helped him win the election. At a swanky New Year's Eve bash at his Mar-a-Lago Club, he drew raucous, extended applause from the black-tie crowd when he recently repeated the vow. Only a dummy wants government in control of healthcare. Johnny B Good would not be good for anybody's healthcare.

One gentleman from Virginia, in a survey recently offered this response:

"It's a welfare program disguised as a health care program," said Charles Kraut, 67, a financial adviser who believes the smaller government is, the better. "Please show me where in the Constitution it says that the government should "promote the general welfare" by stealing from half the population to give to the other half." This gentleman has health insurance through his, but he resents having his tax dollars go things he would never get as options on his health insurance such as sex-change operations and abortions on demand.

Many others say there is nothing affordable about the Affordable Care Act. They resent that they were lied to by the President that premiums would go down and they could choose their own doctors. What they got was high premiums and deductibles that get worse every year. They are also angry that they couldn't keep the insurance plan or doctors that they had. It is not nice for politicians to try to fool the part of the public that pays attention.

Table of Contents

Ch 1 Setting the Table
Congress not interested in Americans or truth

...

After seven years of promising to repeal and replace Obamacare, the verdict is in, at least so far. When Republicans got their chance with a majority in the Senate and the House as well as owning the presidency, they reneged. Their promise to do exactly what they said was a lie of convenience to get elected.

...

Obamacare's repeal is, at least for the foreseeable future, dead. John McCain hates Donald Trump as much as he hates his own word.

The simplest explanation of why the Obamacare effort repeal failed is that McCain's vote — coupled with longstanding opposition from Sens. Lisa Murkowski (R-AK) and Susan Collins (R-ME) — meant that the Health Care Freedom Act could not move through the chamber.

Congress often uses deceit and lies to buffalo the American people. Soon, the buffaloing buffoons will be whistling their way out of their own cozy chairs as the people vote in replacement players. Americans do not like liars.

Ch 2 Ryancare-- No Chance of Becoming Law
Silly Congressional rules must be changed

If we ever accept again a premise that Paul Ryan intends to do what is right for the American people, shame on us? Ryan claimed to put out a premise that he had constructed the best bill possible to repeal and replace Obamacare as he and the Republicans promised to the American people? There were just two things wrong with his bill: It neither repealed nor replaced Obamacare. If we can get past that, and we still think Ryan did his well-intentioned best, then he clearly failed.

If on the other hand as some suggest, Ryan's objective was to snooker the American people while snookering President Trump into thinking the only way to pass anything was to pass his elite establishment concoction euphemistically labeled as The American Healthcare Act of 2017, for a while at least, he accomplished his goal.

The bill was replete with so many twists and turns that it was as if Ryan was hoping that with enough wrong turns, it would bring him to the right place. Unfortunately, few of us were convinced he wanted to take us anyplace good nor anyplace he had promised.

The House bill which Paul Ryan pushed to "repeal and replace" Obamacare quickly became a bill that nobody wanted to own. Tell me folks, do any of us think that fact alone demonstrated enough about this legislation?

Donald Trump, God love him for his energy, was erroneously told by Mr. Ryan that what he saw, was all he could get. He was also told that Mr. Ryan as the Speaker of the House could deliver it as it existed in a binary vote in the House. So much wanting something rather than nothing. The President went for it. He believed Ryan to be a truthful man. More and more see that supposition as a mistake!

There was a major problem causing all the stink. The bill did not accomplish the # 1 objective. It did not repeal Obamacare. How can a repeal and replace bill not do the repeal?

Ch 3 The Simple Solution
Need honest representation

I was very impressed with the work of Jim Jordan on the Obamacare repeal that I sent him a note. It included my plan that demonstrates how easy the process can be.

March 8, 2017
Representative Jim Jordan
3121 West Elm Plaza
Lima, Ohio 45805

Dear Congressman Jordon,

Thank you for asking for the legislation promised to all Americans from Republicans regarding the complete repeal of Obamacare. I agree that what is on the table is not what was promised.

I sent a letter to my home paper, which prescribed a simple solution that Americans would like. I suspect your solution is similar. I send this to you in the event it may help. The parts that were printed in the paper are at this URL:

http://citizensvoice.com/opinion/replacing-obamacare-should-be-simple-1.2163103

The parts that were not printed show that Obamacare affects just 4% of the population. Why we are doing handstands on legislation that can be straightforward is a conundrum for me unless Washington wants to retain control of our healthcare. The entire letter, as sent to the editor, is shown below

Repealing and Replacing Obamacare Should Be Simple:

First of all, the nastiest part of Obamacare is its 20,000+ pages which include the 2700 pages in the legislation and in total about 20,000 pages of regulations. US citizens need to have this onerous burden lifted from our backs.

When we consider that after 7 years, just 4% of the population is "benefiting" from Obamacare, it makes it look like a silly experiment in government buffoonery. The KISS approach should apply here (Keep It Simple, Stupid!).

Why it is taking so long to come up with a solution means government must be trying to keep control. Government should have little to no control and should make a graceful exit from running and controlling American healthcare.

Here are some facts:

Citizen population of the US is now 325 million

- 45 million get insurance from Medicare
- 70 million get insurance from Medicaid and CHIP
- 152 million get insurance from employers
- 13 million get insurance from Obamacare exchanges
- 60 million are either other-insured, self-insured or uninsured.

Under Obamacare, firms with 100 or more full-time equivalent employees (FTE) needed to insure at least 70% of their full-time workers by 2015 and 95% by 2016.

Those with 50 or less employees do not have to pay for employees' insurance. In 2015, 56% of non-elderly residents (270M *.56 = 152M) got their health insurance through work.
About 87% of the 13 million who buy Obamacare through Exchanges are getting some form of cost assistance to cover premiums and deductibles.

Costs and deductibles for those getting no subsistence are huge and unaffordable. For example, Mrs. X, a 63-year old real person recently compared prices for individual health insurance plans and can't believe what she found:

"They cost $1,200 a month, and they have a deductible of $6,000," she said. "I don't know how they think anyone can afford that." Mrs. X lives in Hull, Georgia,

Though it is only 13 million of 325 million right now who are under Obamacare, many citizens fear the government control that comes with Obamacare and its high premiums, poor access, and huge deductibles. Mrs. X will pay over $20,000 before Obamacare buys her a single aspirin.

The 87% who receive cost subsidies when surveyed, report that they are very pleased with Obamacare. This is understandable but not representative of the full population. After all, the rest of us are paying for their subsidies.

Millions like Mrs. X have realized they are too poor for Obamacare. There are lots of reasons why it is so expensive such as silly things like Mrs. X at 63 needs pre-natal care to be included in her policy. Moreover, Mrs. X can only buy insurance from somebody licensed in her state. v

The solution is very simple but just like it took 7 years for President Obama to get us to this point of crisis, it is not an overnight solution. However, with immediate action, the solution can begin immediately. I mean like tomorrow. I would project that in 2 to 2.5 years we can be 100% rid of Obamacare control of healthcare.

Here are the ingredients

1. Repeal Obamacare immediately [Use a one-line repeal] rendering the 2700 original pages of government control, with added regulations reaching 20,000 pages (three feet of paper) obsolete.

2. Begin the transition to a market-based system in two years. No citizens should be harmed during this process. The market system would have no government involvement and non-Obamacare polices, such as those from before 2010; should begin to be written immediately. The changes would include:

A. Permit insurance companies to immediately sell across state lines any policy that provides marketplace healthcare insurance to any potential subscriber. Make it so Obamacare policies may be canceled by the insured at any time during the two-year transition period if desired. No more new Obamacare policies will be issued.

B. Begin a two-year delay before all Obamacare policies are canceled. During this period, all existing healthcare insurance may stay in effect with no more than a 5% per annum increase for those that choose not to change at all. Once the move to a market solution is made by an individual or employer, the two-year hiatus for them is complete.

During the two years, the provision for children on parents' policies and the preexisting conditions stay in effect. Other good rules regarding policy cancellation also continue.

During this two-year period and no longer, the government may have to subsidize this to make up for the past ills of Obamacare.

The government made a big mistake and it is proper that it pay for its mistake until the two-years is up.

C. Those who today receive subsidies for Obamacare, may keep them for the two years. Then, their cases are turned over to the states, and they may receive Medicaid if they qualify.

D. When the two-year wait is up, Medicaid control goes back to the States.

E. When Obamacare is gone in two years. these are the options: Medicare; Medicaid and Chip; Insurance from employer; Private insurance; other-insurance, self-insurance or no insurance.

Sincerely,

Brian W. Kelly

I think that about does it but here is one more thought:

What do the people want?

A one-line repeal bill is all that is needed and then let the Marketplace takeover with a few well-meaning tweaks if necessary. But, just a few!

I am not the first to suggest a very short bill. But, I am the first to suggest a one-line bill.

A great one sentence bill

On March 28, 2017 as reported by Fox News, an Alabama congressman introduced a one-sentence bill in the House Friday to repeal Obamacare. I love that my recommended bill size is smaller, but I am more tickled that there are others that think the charade of repeal and replace has gone on too long. Just repeal.

Let the marketplace replace it!

Mo Brooks has become one of my living heroes

Republican Representative Mo Brooks from Alabama, introduced the bill as the Obamacare Repeal Act.

AL.com reported the big sentence:

"Effective as of Dec. 31, 2017, the Patient Protection and Affordable Care Act is repealed, and the provisions of law amended or repealed by such Act are restored or revived as if such Act had not been enacted,"   The following text would be my one-line repeal:

Obamacare repealed immediately. Specifics to follow.

Don't you just love the tone?

Brooks introduced the bill after he announced that he was against Ryan care, which in its early incarnation, was pulled from a House floor vote because it did not have enough support to pass.

"If the American people want to repeal Obamacare, this is their last, best chance during the 115th Congress," Brooks said in a statement. Those Congressmen who are sincere about repealing Obamacare may prove it by signing the discharge petition…"

"At a minimum, the discharge petition will, like the sun burning away the fog, show American voters who really wants to repeal Obamacare and who merely acts that way during election time."

The bill was not voted on as Paul Ryan considered it a symbolic gesture. Isn't that reflective of why there is little trust in our Congress, especially its leadership.

Mo Brooks constructed and presented a great bill which would not have been a symbolic gesture if Congress wanted to assure that it kept its promise to repeal and replace Obamacare. They could have passed it.

The replace part was implicit as once Obamacare was repealed, insurance companies from all over the world would be flocking like buzzards to the US with the most innovative policies you have ever seen since the beginning of Obamacare.

By the way, though I like my one-line repeal, I would go with Mo Brooks one sentence repeal as it does the same thing.

Chapter 7 Boost Social Security Now!

Brian W. Kelly

Boost Social Security Now!

Hey Buddy, Can You Spare a Dime?

Hey Buddy, Can You Spare a Dime?

Book purpose:

The mainstream economists and the media tend to ignore the truth regarding the consumer price index. The CPI is really not indicative of the actual inflation rate as the Bureau of Labor Statistics (BLS) purports. With too much skin in the game, this government tool has engaged in methodological shenanigans over the past couple decades that are directed at depriving seniors their true cost of living annual increment. This is well documented by John Williams of ShadowStats, among others.

All their monkeying with reality means that the official rate of inflation is listed as two to five times lower than the actual rate. This is very convenient if you are a government bureaucrat trying to hold down interest costs and Social Security payments. It is not such a nice thing for seniors trying to avoid their next home being the poorhouse.

It is not surprising that "deep thinking" coffee-breath professors are on the side of liberals in government rather than the people, including their own grandmothers. Americans depend on the truth for an honest cost of living adjustment—something which has not happened in over thirty years. In other words, the government has been flat out lying to reduce its obligation to seniors.

From my own analysis of the shadowstats.com work, seniors should be receiving amounts that are over 4X their current checks. This is a travesty and must be corrected as more and more seniors are becoming destitute, having to make choices like paying property taxes or buying bread and milk. My recommendation is to right this wrong and not by a generous 2% margin as has been the best in five years. We must immediately boost the COLA rate for 2018 to 15% and to report expenses fairly, we must put Medicare Part B and other health insurance notions into the calculation.

It is puzzling how Medicare can go up by exactly the same amount as the SSR COLA and yet not count in the COLA? The fake CPI put out by the BLS is simply a fraud, and the chained CPI planned for the future is an even greater fraud. The CPI must be corrected, and back pay is well due seniors. If the government fixed the game and began to give 15% a year beginning this year for at least four years, I think most seniors would forgive public officials for their thirty years of chicanery.

Why would a country punish senior citizens?

The most beleaguered citizens in the United States are our senior citizens. Seniors are victims of government fraud. It should not be so; but it is easy to explain. There is not one senior citizen member of Congress, who actually depends on Social Security to make ends meet. How is it then that they get to cast their magic wands annually to determine the cost of living increase due seniors. They feel none of the pain of seniors—none!

Congressional inflation estimates unfortunately are nothing close to the reality of the real price increases seniors actually pay every-day at supermarkets and clothing stores in America? The law on SSR has been distorted and seniors need and deserve a massive adjustment. It is up to seniors to make sure Congress knows that it has not delivered. Perhaps when seniors are the reason for members being sent home for good after the next election, the Congress will understand.

If President Obama had another heart, some say it would be lonesome. For eight years, seniors served as the former President's personal punching bag as he stubbornly refused to give seniors a break. Obama even tried to reduce senior benefits with his chained CPI proposal. Then, he took more than $700 Billion from Medicare to fund his signature legislation known as Obamacare.

Democrats, the ones who claim Republicans have no hearts are all Tin Men on the SSR issue and their main man for eight years, Barack H. Obama had no regard at all for Seniors. He claimed otherwise but worked to reduce SSR benefits for the duration of his eight years in office. He simply could not sneak it in without hurting the Democratic Party, so they stopped him.

Wimpy Republicans without the courage of Donald Trump, permitted the former President to decrease the livelihood of seniors and chose not to fire back at the former president with the gumption they now show when opposing Trump. They chose to do nothing to help seniors.

Mike Huckabee was the first Republican to complain when he publicly accused "illegals, prostitutes, pimps, (and) drug dealers" of freeloading off the Social Security system during the first GOP primary debate way back on August. 6, 2015. This freeloading must be paid back to seniors. Despite President Trump's problems with Republican RINOs, seniors pray he still has the energy to help.

During his campaign, candidate Trump promised to protect Social Security without cutting benefits. I wrote this book to help remind the new President that a huge SSR monthly increase is the right medicine and it must be done ASAP before more seniors suffer.

Seniors, if denied the proper increase, need more than just accepting the bad medicine of the past. They need to be paid back for the abuses to the system over the years that Mike Huckabee and others have cited. If you don't have a mom or a dad who are hurting because their Social Security "check" does not even pay for their meals, you can't know how bad it is in America for "poor" seniors.

What should President Trump do in the absence of any Congressional leadership? His positive actions would include paying back Medicare from Obamacare. It would include increasing SSR benefits over the next four years of the Trump term by at least 15% per year.

Even this will not make up for what was stolen from seniors using a fraudulent cost of living percentage. President Trump knows that revenue flows from elimination of waste, fraud, & abuse and he can direct that American oil reserves can provide ample cash for strategic emergency make-up funding for senior benefits.

What would you pay to see every senior in America smile because buying a fresh loaf of bread and a dozen eggs is no longer a big issue in their lives? Seniors ask for nothing more than to be made whole for the intentional fraud in Congress's CPI calculations and to use an accurate measurement of the cost of living and the out-of-pocket expenses endured by seniors.

My concern is that the good President Trump, as the sitting president, may be so insulated from the reality he knew as a candidate, might sit idle and permit an unfair inflation rate put more and more seniors in the poorhouse.

The President must make up for all the past bad CPIs at once. American can take care of her seniors if we so desire. In this book, we tell you how things can and must be made lots better for penniless seniors, whose scant increases get wiped out all the time by Medicare increases. You'll be surprised as to how much sense the proposal to Boost Social Security now makes. It is the new senior credo and mantra. President Trump cannot let seniors down.

Table of Contents

Preface:

Congress & the President must act now to avoid a bigger crisis!

Somebody will say that the US cannot afford to pay for seniors to be OK! I say that we cannot afford not to do what is right. This is America.

If somebody says we cannot afford to assure that seniors can lead lives in which the poorhouse is not a constant threat, please tell them to read Chapter 11 of Boost Social Security Now from start to finish and use their imagination. America and Americans can do anything we choose to do. We in the Boomer generation learned that growing-up. Unfortunately, that message of truth has been diluted recently by Democrats trying to do nice things for illegal aliens at the expense of seniors.

We can afford making seniors whole again and we must. The dirtiest politicians in America colluded so they would not have to take the real cost of living into consideration for the last thirty years or so. Nobody in America wants this perpetration to stand, especially seniors who just lost their homes and who are now scraping to find a good meal.

My dad, as I grew up in the 1960's told me often that Roosevelt's Social Security was not welfare. He loved Roosevelt's programs to save those who might not be well-off in the future of America as they aged. Everybody had to contribute to SSR, so that all Americans could retire with dignity. The Congress of the USA, shame on them, have brought a period of indignity upon seniors through fraud, and they should be held accountable.

For eight years of President Obama's regime, it was not very safe to be a senior citizen. It is still not safe. President Trump has a mission to learn how poorly seniors in the middle class and lower have been treated by the US government. Many seniors are hopeful things will change.

In former president Obama's heart, he had to know that this batch of seniors did not trust him very much to do the right thing by them. Seniors got exactly what they expected from Obama – nothing. Five zero or almost zero cost of living raises were the order of the day in eight years while Obama seemed to be smiling about the savings he had secured off the backs of seniors.

Only low information seniors, and there are far too many for the good of the US senior citizen population, continued to the end to give the former president the benefit of the doubt. I guess this was because they listened to the corrupt mainstream media and read the biased New York Times.

They may have received lots less than ever before, but they loved President Obama nonetheless. He had the gift of gab and for many, he was a fine pied piper. They would follow him anywhere and they still will even if they die of starvation. My advice for other seniors is start reading to these guys the facts of our nation every day.

The reality is that even today, starving seniors do not fault the former president, though they would if they really knew what he did to them. Worse than that, if they knew how bad he tried to make it, but failed, seniors would be enraged. You'll learn what that was in this book. President Obama did his best to destroy the lives of senior citizens. He knew seniors did not trust them and he was a great guy for a big payback for his detractors.

As noted previously, it is a documented fact that the most beleaguered citizens in the United States today are senior citizens. Why is that and why should it not change immediately with a kinder Trump administration? Some seniors are so respectful of authority that they become dumb when a Democrat suggests they have it made because of all great Democratic programs—even when their cereal bowl is empty in the morning. Unaffordable raisins and other fruit in the cereal bowl should not be on the menu. How about we all try living on that.

For eight years, any senior paying attention, and not part of the love-fest, noticed that they were serving as former President Obama's personal punching bags. He knew that in their hearts, many, who knew what he was up to had little regard for him.

They had him pegged right as a man who would take away their last drop of water if he could—if they promised to die quietly.

They were right. There is lots more inside this book to help seniors move to action to assure that SSR increases are fair and that the government brings seniors back to where they should be—after all the government lying on the inflation rate.

Yes, I am talking about large annual increases in COLA for the next eight years to help seniors get back most of what they lost because of all the fraud associated with the government's cost of living adjustments.

You are going to love this book as it tells it like it is. Feel free to contact your Congressman and President Trump so that they know how you feel. One day we will all be seniors.

I wish you all the best
Brian P. Kelly, Publisher
P.O Box 621 Wilkes-Barre, Pennsylvania 18703

Ch 1 Hey Buddy, Can you Spare a Dime?
2018 SSR Benefits raise for seniors is net of "0"

There is no official abbreviation for social security or social
security retirement. Therefore, in this book we will use our own
abbreviation SSR to mean social security as well as for social
security retirement. As many know, the German Army in World
War II commandeered the term SS and, so we will stay away from
any negative connotation by staying away from that abbreviation.

When President Trump was inaugurated, the paltry increase from
President Obama's last year in office was .3%. That is .003 for
those like me who want to really know where the decimal point is.

I don't think that President Trump intended to slam seniors like
Obama did; but they got slammed nonetheless as Obama's last
approved increment was implemented by the newly elected
President Trump. Seniors who think this President does no wrong
are now hoping he sees what happened throughout the Obama
years and about thirty years before, and that he adjusts things
retroactively to where they should be.

My sources say that the COLA received v the COLA which
should have been applied to senior retirement income is in the
neighborhood of 4X. That means that SSR recipients would be
getting $2000 per month instead of $500.

It may be hard to believe because most Americans would never
think that their precious Congressmen, who they live intrinsically
would ever permit that to happen. When I ran for Congress in
2010, the 26-year, 13-term Congressman I hoped to replace had
already stiffed his senior constituency of about 2.5X of the 4x.
That means if they were getting $500, they should have been
getting at least $1250. As my dad would say once it is gone. "Try
and get it!"

The potential benefits increase for millions of seniors in 2017 was expected to be larger than usual to make up for the past abuses by government in calculating the inflation rate. After Obama's almost-zero last rate at .3%, President Trump's announced rate at 2% for 2018 is admittedly about six times more than the $5 buck raise per month in Obama's swan-song. But, it shows no deference to seniors who feel things the Trump family has never felt.

The paltry increase still does not make up for the actual inflation rate's impact on seniors' income. Moreover, it does nothing to counteract the intentional lowball CPI official inflation rates, endured for over thirty years. These cost seniors many thousands of dollars, even though they were fraudulent. Seniors who do not pay attention to the screwage, need to figure out how to ask for what Roosevelt promised them. Send your Congressman home if he does not reply.

In government the left hand takes what the right hand gives. Seniors in 2017 already got the bad news that Medicare premiums for physicians' services rose again and would rise again in 2018 and again. Thus, Medicare, buy the design of a Congress that gives less than a damn for seniors, will consume the entire cost-of-living adjustment for most seniors for 2018 again.

It is hard to believe that the same government that thinks seniors should get 2% to help with increased costs and out of pocket expenses, is stealing back the 2% for Medicare. Why are such costs not included in the COLA? No government costs which are clearly known are mitigated. Seniors lose again. But why? Hey Buddy, Can You Spare a Dime?

Brother, Can You Spare a Dime? is a 1975 documentary film starring Walt Disney, Bing Crosby, Charlie Chaplin, Andrews Sisters, Fred Astaire, Shirley Temple, Eleanor Roosevelt, and Franklin Delano Roosevelt. It was produced by Image Entertainment, consisting largely of newsreel footage and contemporary film clips to portray the era of the Great Depression and the tough times experience equally by most Americans.

To the rest of the Country, the Trump era is now bringing in prosperity that has been absent for at least eight years. But, not everybody is gaining. Seniors are still suffering through the Great

CPI Depression, with its major inflation tax. So far, there is no recovery in sight.

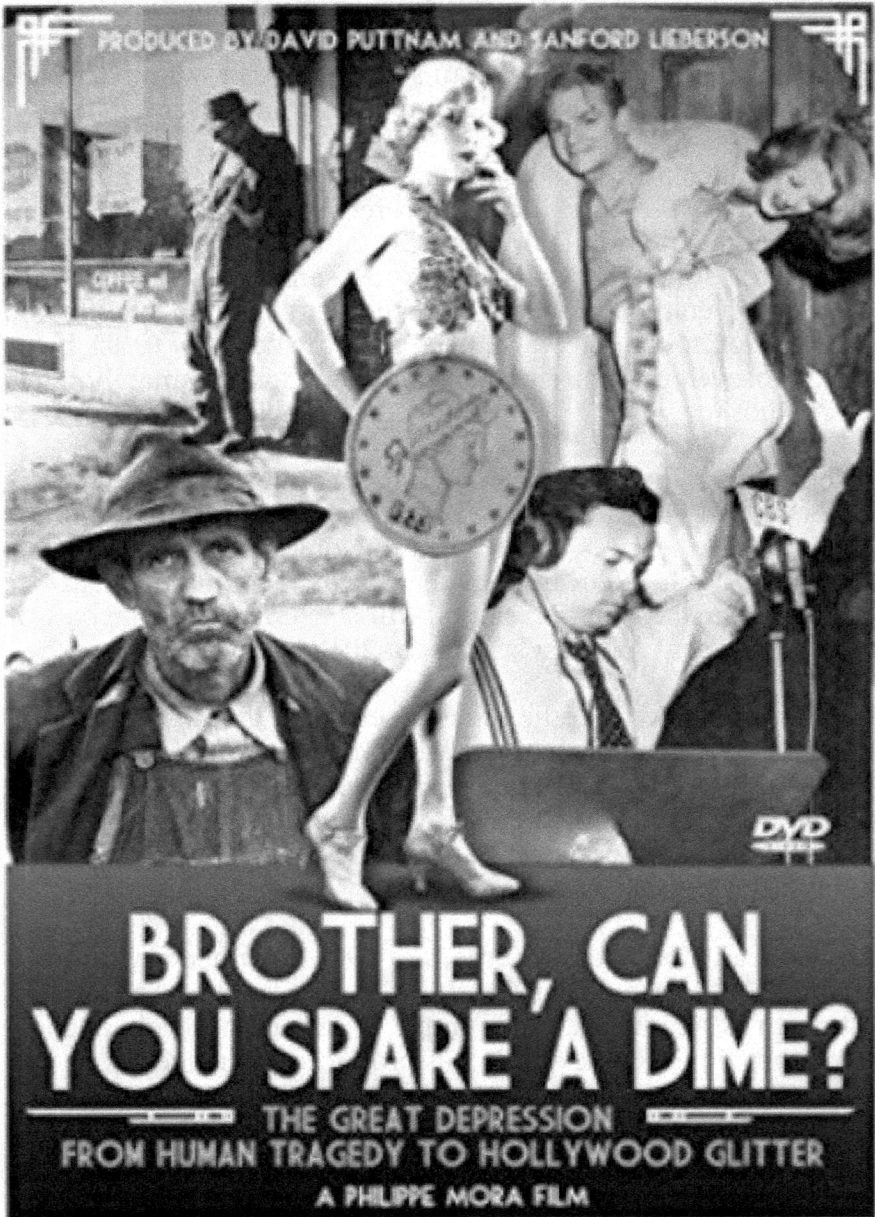

"Brother, Can You Spare A Dime?"

They used to tell me I was building a dream
And so I followed the mob
When there was earth to plow or guns to bear
I was always there, right on the job

They used to tell me I was building a dream
With peace and glory ahead
Why should I be standing in line
Just waiting for bread?

Once I built a railroad, I made it run
Made it race against time
Once I built a railroad, now it's done
Brother, can you spare a dime?

Once I built a tower up to the sun
Brick and rivet and lime
Once I built a tower, now it's done
Brother, can you spare a dime?

Once in khaki suits, gee, we looked swell
Full of that Yankee Doodly Dum
Half a million boots went slogging through Hell
And I was the kid with the drum

Say, don't you remember? They called me 'Al'
It was 'Al' all the time
Why don't you remember? I'm your pal
Say buddy, can you spare a dime?

Once in khaki suits, ah, gee, we looked swell
Full of that Yankee Doodly Dum
Half a million boots went slogging through Hell
And I was the kid with the drum

Oh, say, don't you remember? They called me 'Al'
It was 'Al' all the time
Say, don't you remember? I'm your pal
Buddy, can you spare a dime?

Will Donald Trump come through for seniors?

It gives me no pleasure to say that Donald Trump will get little more than one more year of good will from seniors. In too many ways, today's times for seniors remind me of the peasants rotting in the Russian gulags. Looking for any hope, they found every excuse to forgive Joseph Stalin for their plight. "If only Joseph knew!" They believed 100% that somehow if he only knew, Stalin would do something to help them.

Chapter 6 Wipe Out All Student Loan Debt—Now!

Unique solutions to the $1.45 Trillion debt accumulation

Book purpose:

There are lots better solutions to the problem of seventeen and eighteen-year-olds having been persuaded to dig a huge hole in their lives with no escape simply so that they can attend college. Somehow, the same banks or financial aid offices would not loan a 17-year-old enough to buy a water gun, a bike, or a car and certainly not a house. Yet they are willing to loan a house-worth of cash, so a kid can go to college.

They don't promise a job after four years when they take that $100,000 from the kid. They don't even promise a degree. Worse than that, they don't promise anything close in value to its $100,000 price tag. No wonder 1 out of 6 borrowers default when the time comes to pay back the loan. And, the rate of defaults is getting even worse.

More than half of the 45 million former student borrowers are struggling to pay back $1.45 trillion. The big winners in the rigged student loan game are the universities and the loan sharks. Instead of student-loan bankruptcy being against the law it ought to be against the law to give so much money to a kid who cannot make a living after graduation. We all know that sociology majors, no matter whether they get a prized $20,000 per year job or not are going to be struggling all their lives in such a crowded field. Yes, it ought to be against the law.

The more I researched this topic the more I felt that students have been fraudulently abused by big Universities, big loan sharks, and the big Obama era student loan officials. Elizabeth Warren on Saturday, September 26th, 2015 in a speech about Obama's takeover of student loans blasted his administration for being piggy by charging usury-level interest rates.

It seems that student loans from the federal government issued between 2007 and 2012 are on target "to produce $66 billion in profits for the United States government." So, not only is the government ripping off student borrowers on the loans, they are making a big profit, the purpose of which of course is to help fund Obamacare.

I once thought this problem could be solved by a combination of lower interest rates, some forgiveness, etc. I no longer think a piecemeal plan is the correct solution. Why did I change my perspective?

I fear that an entire generation of students, mostly millennials, will be lost and will never be found again unless drastic action is taken now. And so, I call for legislation that wipes out all student debt now. Wait until you see what such an act does to boost our economy beyond expectations. In this book, I offer some great ways in which we can pay for the write-off without hurting taxpayers.

President Trump knows a ripoff & a rigged system

President Trump in understandable terms has netted out the student debt crisis from both a student and parent perspective: "They go, and they work, and they take loans, and they're borrowed up, and they can't breathe, and they get through college and the worst thing is, they go through that whole process and they don't have any job." Trump has it right, and worse than that, when the US system hurts them, our best and brightest lose hope.

Many have excoriated the Obama Administration and government and coffee-breath professors who teach nothing, for making it worse for college graduates. They all make money on the student loan program. Trump says: "You know the one program that the U.S. makes a whole lot of money with is student loans, and that's maybe the one program they shouldn't be making money with… "So, we're going to have to start a program," he said. "We're going to do something very big with loans because you have to get these people going. They really feel down and out."

Donald J. Trump is right. Yet he is the only president who has even talked about solving America's problem with rip-off loan sharks and a government that makes big money off the backs of student borrowers. Ironically, the man willing to help is hated by the very young Americans he speaks about helping.

College graduates and those former students not fortunate enough to complete their degrees need all the help they can get to claw their way out of their college debt. Your author as a professor and as a father understands student debt. He feels and has intellectually analyzed the plight and the pain felt by today's millennials. Besides recommending a total forgiveness and a do-again, this book also examines other ways to solve the problem including refinancing, extending, and providing better payment plans as well as getting universities to put some skin in the game.

This book addresses the massive $1.45 Trillion student debt already on the books and it presents a boldly unique plan to assure that students with loans have a chance of success with a job of their choice. Isn't it about time? This book tells you how it can be done. You won't be able to put this book down before you know what you can do to help those with student debt be able to afford homes and start families and live the life of a real American and not an indentured servant.

Preface:

Rarely does a book title explain exactly what a book is about. This book is the exception. Wiping out all student loan debt now will immediately solve the student debt crisis. There is no question about it.

It will also kick start the economy with such a punch that Americans will be talking about how great it is that America is so great again. Additionally, it will bring back a whole generation of lost souls with no chance in life—the millennials—so they can lead normal lives like all other generations before them.

It helps to recall that President Obama increased the National Debt by $9.1 Trillion in just eight years, hoping to assure that illegal aliens had all the resources they needed to take as many American jobs as they could. He just about doubled our debt and has nothing to show. Tell me where the money went? It was spent but what good did it do?

What if we had taken a small piece of that expenditure and paid off all student debt? Wow! What if at the same time so it never happens again, we put in measures to assure that 17-year olds could never be sucked into giving up the promise of a real life for a fake-news promise of prosperity ever, ever again.

It is too bad that he did not have the foresight to use $1.3 Trillion of that wasteful largesse to help America. With less than 15% of this reckless, aimless crony capitalist spending, the former president could have been a folk hero among many Americans.

He could have and should have spent more wisely and wiped out 100% of the student debt now strangling our young American adults and holding the US economy hostage. Until the student debt crisis is put behind us, the most physically capable and more than likely, the brightest people in America, our recent college graduates between the ages of twenty and forty, will not be part of the American game of life.

They will not be in a position to start a business, buy a home, new appliances, a new car, or begin a family. I am talking about 45 million student loan borrowers—seventy percent of all college students / graduates. At a time that we needed Obama's leadership the most, right after the sub-prime mortgage crisis when the economy was at a standstill, how could the former president have missed the opportunity to reinvigorate the economy by freeing 45 million young people from debtor's prison.

The former president had the opportunity to reinsert forty-five million Americans with a propensity to spend money into the economy and he did not choose to act. He chose not to free them from the shackles of repaying a massive and unfair student debt load that will keep them out of the economy for years and years to come.

This book tells Congress and the new president how to solve the crisis and it tells Americans that nothing happens without a vigilant population. That means we must hold our government and our politicians accountable for solving this crisis that affects almost every family in America.

More and more Americans, even those of us who have paid off all of our student debt are looking at today's student loan dilemma much differently. The groundswell of concern for removing so many potentially productive Americans from the economy at one time is at an all-time high with more Americans asking Washington to forgive this debt so that young Americans can engage and so that the economy can be jump-started to make all Americans successful.

Young Americans are literally choking on their student debt. It has their lives stopped and each year that it not solved is another day in a veritable debtor's prison. It is so bad that 50% in a recent survey would be willing to give up their most fundamental freedom to be able to lead a normal life.

A survey from Credible, conducted through Pollfish, hits the seriousness of the situation right on the head. It is understandable that young Americans would want a chance in life by having their debt removed. But it was surprising to many what they would be willing to do to be free of those loans. The most popular answer the 500 respondents between the ages of 18 and 34 chose for what they would be desperate enough to sacrifice was "suffrage." Yes, half surveyed said they would give up the ability to vote in the next two presidential elections to be able to move their lives forward.

It is not just those who would be set free who feel forgiving student debt is an idea whose time has come. More Americans believe that the US should forgive all federal student debt than feel that the recipients should pay their loans back. The results to many of the survey conducted by MoneyTips.com were shocking. Nearly 42% agreed with the statement, "I believe President Trump's Department of Education should forgive all federal student debt to help the economy."

Those who paid off their student debts on time with no issue have a right to be upset by the thought of others getting such a huge break. I paid off my own student debt without help from anybody else. But the amount was nothing like the life-ending loans that today's millennials face. So, many default, and they basically end their lives despite in many cases having a college degree.

So, I asked myself if it helped me in anyway if somebody else got a break in life. Let's say they may have been sucked in at 17 years of age by an admissions counsellor with a big quota who never would have loaned the kid $300 of their own money for a junk car. Yet, they had no problem taking taxpayer funded loans and giving these kids $100,000 and a promise of a great life—a life that never happened for far too many. How would it hurt me if they were helped?

Less than 37% disagreed, while the remaining 21% neither agreed nor disagreed. Some of those who disagreed are hard-core about it as they struggled and paid their loans back but again, why keep somebody poor who made just one bad choice in life.

Even those who for years were pressuring Congress to do the right thing were taken back by the overwhelming response to help these former kids become adults. For example, Brandon Yahn, founder of "studentloanguy.com said: "It is surprising that the majority of the US population supports this measure...Perhaps this student debt burden has spread more across all generations, and popular sentiment is turning the corner as it relates to student debt."

What country would wipe out opportunity for almost a full generation of its citizens when the Congress itself is partially responsible for the easy money these kids spent on an education that brought them no benefits.

When asked further about the positive impact on the economy and the impact of future student's ability to attend college in the future, most believe that this is a one and done. There should never be another forgiveness. And, so the consensus is that there needs to be a fool-proof solution for new student debt so that new high school aspirants to college do not sign up for debt when they do not need to do so.

There are a number of notions in this book besides wiping out all of the (now) $1.45 Trillion. This book discusses most if not all of the theories about how this happened and how it can be made to never happen again. Additionally, it discusses a number of student resources and a few tricks that are both honest and long overdue.

Why did Brian W. Kelly write this book?

Brian W. Kelly wrote this book because he cares about college graduates being able to move on with their lives. I am publishing this book because I care. This book identifies the most notable and most serious flaws in student tuition financing. It then solves them by prescribing a number of Kelly-unique solutions to help get the program back on track.

I hope you enjoy this book and I that it inspires you to take the individual actions necessary to help the government of the US stand firm against any attacks on democracy from outside or from within this great country. A great start of course is to stop the government gouging of young Americans, who are plagued with student debt. Instead government should be a helpful tool in solving this deep moral dilemma for our country.

I wish you the best.
Brian P. Kelly, Publisher
Wilkes-Barre, Pennsylvania

Table of Contents:

Ch 1 The Best Student Debt Solution
Congress must have the will to act

There are many solutions for student loan debt at different levels discussed in this book. The first and the best solution is depicted in the title of the book: Wipe Out All Student Loan Debt Now! It is clearly the ideal solution from an American point of view and it has economic ramifications that along with the new tax plan can add to a major jump re-starting of the economy. The ideal solution would be to wipe out all of the student debt from all college loans. There are many ways the US can afford this and prosper because of it.

This act alone would free forty-five million debt-ridden former college students, mostly graduates to go ahead and get real lives for themselves. They will be in a position to start a business, buy a home, a new car, and begin a family.

The negative impact of so many student borrowers is clear. Essentially, the US has 45 million Americans, who are putting a big chunk of their monthly income towards their student debts. That means that they aren't spending on other economy-boosting goods or services. This group also has less money to save, invest, or even start a business. The burden is so heavy that over 8 million (and growing) have stopped paying a dime. This phenomenon is called being in default.

Three other Opinions on canceling Student Loan Debt

I am not the only person who thinks it is a good idea to start over again on student loans and wipe what we have off the books as soon as possible. Here are three other opinions as to why it is not only a good idea; it is a great idea and the US can not only afford it; the country will profit from it.

David Muccigrosso, an Armchair Economist, blogging at //www.quora.com, on Feb 12, 2013 took a shot at answering this important question: What would be the economic impact of forgiving all US student loan debt?

At the time this was written in 2013, student loans and debt in the US exceeded credit card debt, at just over $1 trillion. Now the debt is closer to $1.45 trillion because there have been no major changes made by colleges and universities to assure new student debtors will be able to pay back their loans. Here is David's piece:

"Around 80% of that is guaranteed by the federal government, with the rest belonging to private lenders.

"Theoretically, winding down all student loan debt would proceed like a national, publicly organized bankruptcy. The federal government would start by forcing lenders to take a "haircut" (significant discount to outstanding principle) on the loans it's guaranteed, and it would allow private loans to be consolidated as federal loans for the purpose of being put through this program as well.

"Winding down $1 trillion in debt is hard in any circumstance. This will be even harder given the sheer amount of bitching the financial sector already does about the federal government. The program would probably take from $500 to $800 billion in total spending (equating to a 50-20% haircut for investors) - roughly the same magnitude as the Bush stimulus package.

"Most banks would not be crippled, but the financial sector would still have a hard time dealing with the hit to their balance sheets...

"The other major problem would be that a program of this magnitude would destroy the student lending market as we know it. Higher education finance would have to be replaced by a spending package on the order of at least $1 trillion and involving some higher taxes to provide free universal public higher education - the only real option once you've taken debt-financed education off the table. (TBH, I'm actually in favor of a less dramatic version of this whole wind-down and conversion, but this incarnation is just too unworkable)

"On the plus side, those suffering under student loan burdens would have a lot of income freed up. You'd probably see surges in multifamily unit construction (apt buildings), the auto industry, and nightlife/entertainment spending, but the economic activity wouldn't cancel out the huge Wall Street "shit fit" that would be simultaneously occurring.

Forgive student loan debt to stimulate the economy.

Originally Written – January 29, 2009
By – Robert Applebaum at http://studentdebtcrisis.org

Back in 2009, President Obama signed into law a $787 billion stimulus package on top of Bush's grossly mismanaged $700 billion TARP bailout from September. That is more than the total student debt of today, $1.45 trillion.

Shortly thereafter in 2009, the Federal Reserve basically printed an additional $1,000,000,000,000 to inject more funds into the monetary system, which will undoubtedly have the effect of diminishing the purchasing power of the dollar. Now, we are approaching twice the total of all the student debt. In other words, if we acted then to forgive the debt, it would be all gone, and all paid for.

Since then, the US government has paid out trillions of dollars in bailouts, handouts, loans and giveaways, with no end in sight as our leaders tried to do anything and everything to get our spiraling economy under control. While some of what Washington has already done may act to stimulate the economy, much of the trillions of dollars already spent will, no doubt, has proven to be just money wasted.

Tax rebate checks **do not** stimulate the economy – history shows that people either spend such rebates on paying off credit card debt, or they simply save them, doing little to nothing to stimulate the economy. Presumably, that is why they were removed from the final version of the stimulus bill.

The tax cuts that were included, however, amount to a whopping $44 per month for the rest of 2009, decreasing to an even more staggering $33 per month in 2010. This is hardly "relief" as it is likely to help nobody.

The Wall Street financial institutions, auto manufacturers, insurance companies and countless other irresponsible actors received TRILLIONS of taxpayer dollars (as demonstrated above, that's a number with *12* zeros at the end of it) to bail them out of their self-created mess. This, too, did nothing to stimulate the economy. It merely rewarded bad behavior and did nothing to encourage institutional change.

There is a better way

How many times have we heard from our leaders in Washington that education is the key to solving all of our underlying societal problems? The so-called "Silver Bullet." For decades, presidents, senators and members of Congress have touted themselves as champions of education, yet they've done nothing to actually encourage the pursuit of one on an individual level.

Some of us have taken advantage of Federal Stafford Loans and other programs, including private loans, to finance higher education, presumably with the understanding that an advanced degree equates with higher earning power in the future. Many of us go into public service after attaining such degrees, something that's also repeatedly proclaimed as something society should encourage.

Yet, the debt we've accrued to obtain such degrees have crippled our ability to reap the benefits of our educations, causing many to make the unfortunate choice of leaving public service so as to earn enough money to pay off that debt.

Our economy is still in the tank, though with Trump already we are seeing great signs of relief. There isn't a reasonable economist alive who doesn't believe that the economy has needed a real stimulus for a real long time.

The only debate now centers on how to go about doing it. While the new stimulus plan contains some worthy provisions, very little of it will have a significant and immediate stimulating effect on the economy. The Obama Administration itself in 2009, did not expect to see an upsurge in the economy until mid-to-late 2010.

Instead of funneling billions, if not trillions of additional dollars to banks, financial institutions, insurance companies and other institutions of greed that are responsible for the current economic crisis, why is not a better idea to allow educated, hardworking, middle-class Americans to get something in return? After all, they're our tax dollars too!

Forgiving student loan debt would have an immediate stimulating effect on the economy. With Trump, we are already back to 3.3% GDP growth. Who knows what having 45 million ready to spend, millennials reengaged in the economy will do for the country?

Responsible people who did nothing other than pursue a higher education would have hundreds, if not thousands of extra dollars per month to spend, fueling the economy now.

Those extra dollars being pumped into the economy would have a multiplying effect, unlike many of the provisions of the 2009 era stimulus packages. As a result, tax revenues would go up, the credit markets would unfreeze, and many jobs will be created. Consumer spending accounts for over two thirds of the entire U.S. economy and in 2009, consumer spending has declined at alarming, unprecedented rates. Therefore, it stands to reason that the fastest way to revive our ailing economy is to do something drastic to get consumers to spend.

This proposal would quickly revitalize the housing market, the ailing automobile industry, travel and tourism, durable goods and countless other sectors of the economy because the very people who sustain those sectors will automatically have hundreds or, in some cases, thousands of extra dollars per month to spend.

The driving factor in today's economy is fear. Unless and until the middle class feels comfortable enough that they'll have their jobs, health insurance and extra money to spend not only next month, but the month after that, etc., the economy will not, indeed, cannot grow fast enough to stop the hemorrhaging.

Let me be clear. This is not about a free ride. This is about a new approach to economic stimulus, nothing more. To those who would argue that this proposal would cause the banking system to collapse or make student loans unavailable to future borrowers, please allow me to respond. I am in no way suggesting that the lending institutions who carry such debts on their balance sheets get legislatively shafted by having them wiped from their books.

The banks and other financial institutions have already gotten their money regardless because, in addition to the $700 TARP bailout, even more bailout money came their way. This proposal merely suggests that in return for the Trillions of dollars that has been and will continue to be handed over to the banks, educated, hardworking Americans who are saddled with student loan debt should get some relief as well, rather than sending those institutions another enormous blank check.

Because the banks are being handed trillions of dollars anyway, there would be no danger of making funds unavailable to future borrowers.

To avoid the moral hazard that this plan could potentially create, going forward, the way higher education in this country is financed MUST be reformed. Requiring students to amass enormous debt just to receive an education is an untenable approach, as demonstrated by the ever-growing student loan default rates.

Having a loan-based system rather than one based on grants and scholarships or, ideally, public funding, has, over time, begun to have the unintended consequence of discouraging people from seeking higher education at all. That is no way for America to reclaim the mantle of the land of opportunity.

A well-educated workforce benefits society as a whole, not just the students who receive a higher education. It is often said that an undergraduate degree today is the equivalent of a high school diploma 30 or 40 years ago. Accepting the premise as true that society does, in fact, place the same value on an undergraduate degree today as it did on a HS diploma 30 or 40 years ago, then what is the rationale for cutting off public funding of education after the 12th grade?

It seems to me that there is some dissonance in our values that needs to be reconciled. That, however, cannot come to pass until the millions of us already shackled with student loan debt are freed from the enormous economic burdens we're presently carrying.

Many of the vocal nay-sayers to this proposal seem intent on ignoring the fact that Washington will continue to spend trillions of dollars, likely in the form of handing blank checks over to more and more banks, as a way of getting the economy under control. Normative assessments of how things should be, are fine, but they don't reflect reality.

Accepting the premise that Washington will spend Trillions of dollars in unprecedented ways (a good portion of which will just be trial and error, since we're in uncharted waters), what is the argument against directly helping middle class people who are struggling, rather than focusing solely on the banks and other financial institutions responsible for the crisis to begin with?

Further accepting that there is an aggregate amount of outstanding student loan debt totaling approximately $550 Billion, (that's Billion with a B, not a T), [even more in 2017] one is forced to ask again, what is the objection to helping real people with real hardships when all we're talking about is a relative drop in the bucket as compared with what will be spent to dig us out of this hole?

In a perfect world, I share these biases towards personal responsibility and having people pay back what they owe and making good on the commitments they've made. But we don't live in a perfect world and the global economy, not just the U.S. economy, is in a downward spiral, the likes of which nobody truly knows how to fix.

This proposal will immediately free up money for hardworking, educated Americans, giving them more money in their pockets every month, addressing the very real psychological aspects of the recession as much as the financial ones. Is it the only answer? No, of course not. But could it help millions of hardworking people who struggle every month to get by? Absolutely. Support real change we can believe in!

More Americans Want to Forgive Trillion-Dollar Student Loan Debt Than Want It Repaid

MoneyTips http://www.ajc.com
4:00 p.m. Friday, July 21, 2017 Business and Money news

More Americans believe that we should forgive all federal student debt than feel that the recipients should pay their loans back. In a shocking survey recently conducted by MoneyTips.com, nearly 42% agreed with the statement, I believe President Trump's Department of Education should forgive all federal student debt to help the economy. Less than 37% disagreed, while the remaining 21% neither agreed nor disagreed.

"It is surprising that the majority of the US population supports this measure," says Brandon Yahn, Founder of studentloansguy.com. "Perhaps this student debt burden has spread more across all generations, and popular sentiment is turning the corner as it relates to student debt."
…
While income wasn't a factor, gender seemed to affect people's feelings on this subject, with more women favoring forgiveness over men. 47% of the women agreed or strongly agreed with the statement, while less than 36% of the men felt the same way.
…
Reasoned millennial money expert Stefanie O'Connell, "Women are now more likely than men to get a college degree, which may explain why they would favor student loan forgiveness at higher rates. They're also likely to experience career interruptions due to childbearing and caretaking, which can impede their lifetime earning potential and, consequently, their ability to pay back their loans.

Finally, many of the lucrative jobs that don't require a college degree tend to be in male-dominated fields - carpentry, electrical, etc. - which might explain why more women favor loan forgiveness."
…
Says Student Loan Hero, expert Miranda Marquit, "Many millennials, who thought they were doing the right thing, took on student loan debt only to graduate to an economy where jobs have been scarce, and wages have been mostly stagnant for decades. Gone are the days when you could work for the summer and pay for the following school year.

As a society, we sold a dream and failed to deliver. You can make payments on your loans for decades and barely make headway." Adds Marquit:

"As a result, these millennials are unable to help the economy in other ways. Research indicates they are putting off financial milestones that come with economy-building benefits.

"All the consumption that comes with things like buying homes and starting families is being lost because the largest generation yet doesn't have money to spare. Student loan forgiveness would go a long way toward helping millennials feel stable enough to take the next steps in their financial lives, as well as even starting businesses."

Ch 2 No Problem Is Without a Solution
The government is not your friend

Despite self-serving governmental, political, and academic apologists suggesting that there is no real student debt crisis, just ask a recent millennial graduate when they hope to start a family. You better have a lot of time. We keep hearing about a student debt crisis. Yet, politicians continue to argue that there is no student debt crisis though everybody else knows that there is. Perhaps the definition of a crisis can tell us--a time of intense difficulty, trouble, or danger.

The fact is that recent students with major loans are having trouble paying them back. The fact is that they have put off major life plans until their personal crisis improves to manageable.

Is the country in crisis? Whether the country is in crisis or not, taxpayers are now on the hook for about $1.45 trillion outstanding in student debt. That makes student debt substantially larger even than credit card debt. Moreover, it's not looking like it's going to get any better in the future. The graduating class of 2017 owed an average of over $37,000, up from less than $30,000 in 2014.

...

In its #issues 2012 of American Voices, in a piece by Maureen Tkacik of Reuters titled: The student loan crisis that can't be gotten rid of, from August 15, 2012. In this snippet, piece, you get to see three situations where there was a clear abuse of power by the thug student loan collection industry.

"A military veteran sharing his story with Occupy Student Debt has paid $18,000 on a $2,500 loan, and Sallie Mae claims he still owes $5,000; the husband of a social worker bankrupt and bedridden after a botched surgery tells Student Loan Justice of a $13,000 college loan balance from the 1980s that ballooned to $70,000. A grandmother subsisting on Social Security has her payments garnished to pay off a $20,000 loan balance resulting from a $3,500 loan she took out 10 years ago, before she underwent brain surgery." How is this fair? Is this what Congress actually wants?

Ms. Tkacik strengthens her case for some compassion by Congress below:

"You have probably mentally cataloged the student loan crisis alongside all the other looming trillion-dollar crises busy imperiling civilization but also enrich the already rich."

"But it is different from those crises in a few significant ways, starting with the fact that the entire loan business is arguably unconstitutional. You don't have to take it from me: A pre-eminent bankruptcy scholar made precisely this argument under oath before Congress."

"In December 1975, when Congress was debating the first law that made student loans non-dischargeable in bankruptcy, University of Connecticut law professor Philip Shuchman testified that students: 'should not be singled out for special and discriminatory treatment. I have the further very literal feeling that this is almost a denial of their right to equal protection of the laws ... Nor do I think has any evidence been presented that these people, these young people just beginning their years on the whole should be singled out for special and as I view it discriminatory treatment. I suggest to you that this may at least in spirit be a denial of their right to equal protection with the virtual pole star of our constitutional ambit.' "

Ch 3 Is Student Loan Game Rigged?
Do Colleges & Universities have unfair advantages?

You bet they do!

It costs Academic Institutions nothing when students come out sacked with a lifetime of debt after four to six years with no jobs. Donald Trump can recognize a rigged game better than any man in America. He can sniff them out and call them out and /or play against them and still win. He thinks the student loan game is rigged against students and it favors the universities and the government disguised as loan sharks.

Trump does not like that the game is rigged, and he has promised to fix it. The President believes that Universities must have some skin in the game for any long-term solutions to be built.

Many people are affected by the crisis and, so it is a topic at the dinner table in many homes—especially in those homes in which the student loan invoices are beginning to arrive from junior's or missy's four or five-year past sojourn into campus life.

When people in the US discuss the student debt crisis, most focus on how it affects them personally. If they are not directly affected, they discuss the rapid growth in outstanding debt and its impact on the economy and the country.

They may also discuss some of the recent milestones, which are not very positive. For example, student loan debt exceeded credit card debt in 2010 and it exceeded auto loan debt in 2011. It is rapidly rising, and it passed the $1 trillion mark in 2012. It is currently at about $1.45 trillion and growing.

It is a big problem. The Wall Street Journal recently reported that More than 40% of student loan borrowers are either in default, delinquency or have postponed repaying their student loans. It is a crisis and having the federal government making over $45 billion off the backs of student borrowers in excessive interest payments does nothing to help matters.

With about 40% of students defaulting on their loan paybacks— mostly because the payments are so large, is a problem for all

America. It is also a big disgrace for a country that does not want to be labeled as "Third World."

These milestones don't tell us much about the impact of all that debt on the students themselves. Seventeen and Eighteen-year-olds are making lifetime decisions even today with little counselling other than "Don't Worry! Be Happy!"

These naïve high school seniors were originally told by a friendly College Financial Aid Officer that everybody borrows, and it is a privilege to be able to attend this college with the help of the university's loan package.

Does that sound familiar. If Joe's Hot Car Lot was scamming young adults at the same rate as academia, the Justice Department would shut them down. At least Joe's Hot Cars can make it around the block. What about the kids with $50,000 in debt, no degree, and no job?

Sometimes as learned by default interviews, there was never an up-front discussion of the loan impact when it came time to repay it. As hard as it is to believe, the loans came so easy that 53% of the students when graduating, did not even know there was a payback. And we all know what payback is!
...

70% of all college students have borrowed and many who are already enrolled still have more to borrow before they finish their degrees and then have to pay for their college education. It is a national travesty.
...

Can you imagine the major spark in the economy if all of a sudden, millennials became the big spenders and were enabled to throw house parties in homes they never thought they would own?

The fact that Obama's government made about $43 Billion a year in many years, by charging higher than reasonable interest rates on student loans shows that solving the debt problem was never a priority during the last eight years. Let's hope Mr. Trump looks past Obama to create a system that works.

Other books by Brian Kelly: (amazon.com, and Kindle)

Boost Social Security Now! Hey Buddy Can You Spare a Dime?
The Birth of American Football. From the first college game in 1869 to the last Super Bowl
Obamacare: A One-Line Repeal Congress must get this done.
A Wilkes-Barre Christmas Story A wonderful town makes Christmas all the better
A Boy, A Bike, A Train, and a Christmas Miracle A Christmas story that will melt your heart
Pay-to-Go   America-First Immigration Fix
Legalizing Illegal Aliens Via Resident Visas Americans-first plan saves $Trillions. Learn how!
60 Million Illegal Aliens in America!!! A simple, America-first solution.
The Bill of Rights By Founder James Madison Refresh *your knowledge of the specific rights for all*
Great Players in Army Football Great Army Football played by great players..
Great Coaches in Army Football Army's coaches are all great.
Great Moments in Army Football Army Football at its best.
Great Moments in Florida Gators Football Gators Football from the start. This is the book.
Great Moments in Clemson Football CU Football at its best. This is the book.
Great Moments in Florida Gators Football Gators Football from the start. This is the book.
The Constitution Companion. A Guide to Reading and Comprehending the Constitution
The Constitution by Hamilton, Jefferson, & Madison – Big type and in English
PATERNO: The Dark Days After Win # 409. Sky began to fall within days of win # 409.
JoePa 409 Victories: Say No More! Winningest Division I-A football coach ever
American College Football: The Beginning From before day one football was played.
Great Coaches in Alabama Football Challenging the coaches of every other program!
Great Coaches in Penn State Football the Best Coaches in PSU's football program
Great Players in Penn State Football The best players in PSU's football program
Great Players in Notre Dame Football The best players in ND's football program
Great Coaches in Notre Dame Football The best coaches in any football program
Great Players in Alabama Football from Quarterbacks to offensive Linemen Greats!
Great Moments in Alabama Football AU Football from the start. This is the book.
Great Moments in Penn State Football PSU Football, start--games, coaches, players,
Great Moments in Notre Dame Football ND Football, start, games, coaches, players
Cross Country With the Parents A great trip from East Coast to West with the kids
Seniors, Social Security & the Minimum Wage. Things seniors need to know.
How to Write Your First Book and Publish It with CreateSpace
The US Immigration Fix--It's all in here. Finally, an answer.
I had a Dream IBM Could be #1 Again The title is self-explanatory
WineDiets.Com Presents The Wine Diet Learn how to lose weight while having fun.
Wilkes-Barre, PA; Return to Glory Wilkes-Barre City's return to glory
Geoffrey Parsons' Epoch... The Land of Fair Play Better than the original.
The Bill of Rights 4 Dummmies! This is the best book to learn about your rights.
Sol Bloom's Epoch …Story of the Constitution The best book to learn the Constitution
America 4 Dummmies! All Americans should read to learn about this great country.
The Electoral College 4 Dummmies! How does it really work?
The All-Everything Machine Story about IBM's finest computer server.
ThankYou IBM! This book explains how IBM was beaten in the computer marketplace by neophytes

Brian has written 146 books in total. Other books can be found at amazon.com/author/brianwkelly